Animals of the Bible
from A to Z

For Liam and Veronica Mautner,
because I promised your mom I'd help you grow in faith.
(Aunt Alice)

To my parents, Bob and Sue Showalter,
whose love and support have kept me drawing and dreaming.
(Sarah)

ANIMALS OF THE BIBLE FROM A TO Z
Text by Alice Camille
Illustrations by Sarah Evelyn Showalter

Edited by Gregory F. Augustine Pierce
Cover Design by Tom A. Wright
Text design and typesetting by Patricia A. Lynch

Published by ACTA Publications, 5559 W. Howard Street, Skokie, IL 60077-2621, (800) 397-2282, www.actapublications.com.

Library of Congress Catalog number: 2007926287

ISBN-10: 0-87946-331-7
ISBN-13: 978-0-87946-331-1

Printed in the Republic of South Korea

Year 15 14 13 12 11 10 09 08 07
Printing 15 14 13 12 11 10 9 8 7 6 5 4 3 2 First

Animals of the Bible
from A to Z

Text by Alice Camille

Illustrations by Sarah Evelyn Showalter

acta
PUBLICATIONS

A
is for the animals
   that God declared are good.

B is for the bear
    that learns to be a better neighbor.

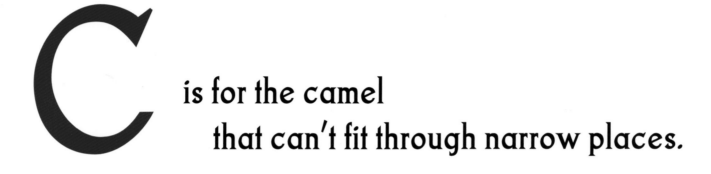

C is for the camel
that can't fit through narrow places.

D is for the dog that walked
the road with young Tobias.

E is for the elephants
    that fought in many battles.

F is for the fish that broke the nets,
there were so many.

G is for the goat that takes
the whole town's blame away.

H

is for the horses
that obey the Lord alone.

I is for the insects that will eat
when God says, "Eat!"

J is for the jackals.
  (They take cities that go bad.)

K is for the kites
    that will not be without their mates.

L is for the lions
    that spared Daniel in their den.

M is for the mice
    that made the Philistines unhappy.

N is for the nestlings
so encouraged by their parents.

 is for the ox
that let the baby use her manger.

P

is for the pigs
   that ran the demons out of town!

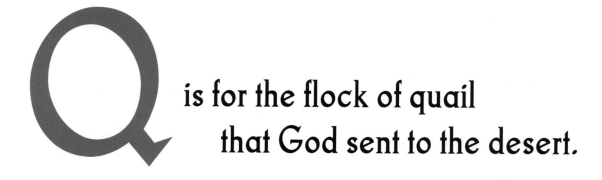

Q is for the flock of quail
that God sent to the desert.

R is for the ravens
that brought food to good Elijah.

S

is for the sheep that's lost
– and Jesus brings him home.

T is for the turtledoves
heard cooing through the land.

U

And if there WAS a Unicorn,
he must have missed the boat....

V is for the vipers
that resemble nasty folks.

is for the great big whale
that swallowed Jonah whole.

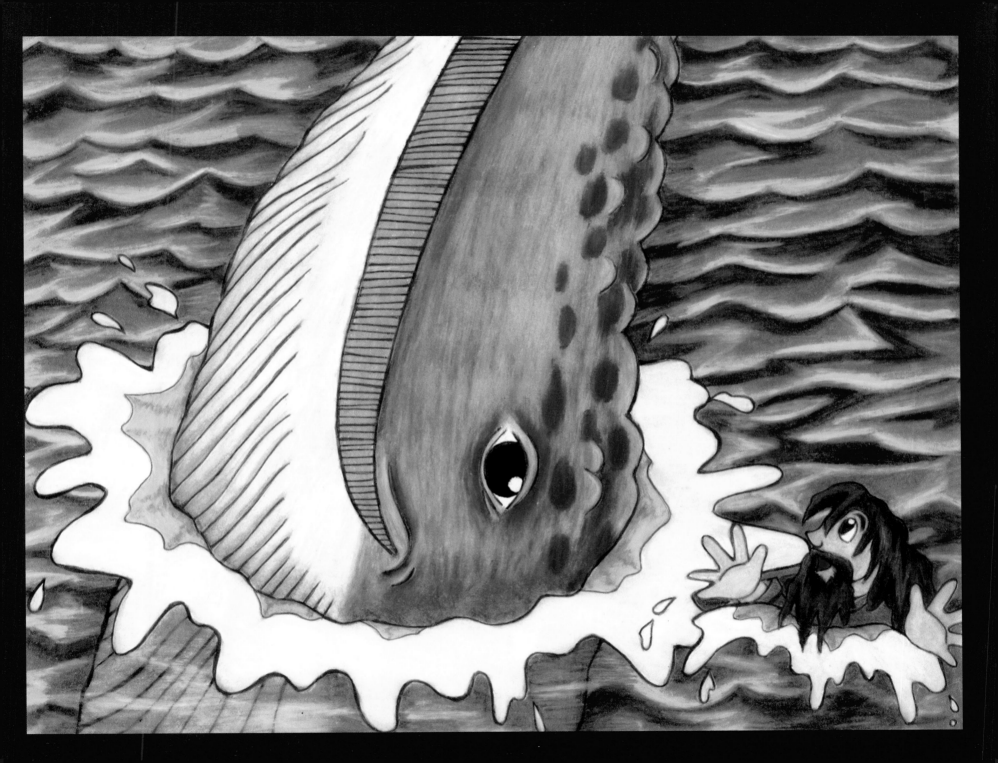

 is for the extra-special donkey
that could talk!

Y is for the yearling lamb
that gave his life like Jesus.

Z is for the zebra pair
    that made it just in time.

PAGES FOR GROWNUPS

Welcome to the back of the book. Here grownups will find help in locating the animals of the Bible found in these pages. Some animals are from familiar Bible stories and need no introduction. Others may be trickier to pinpoint or entirely unfamiliar. Parents, grandparents, and teachers may appreciate suggestions on using these animal stories in the religious education of children. Both Scripture citations and sample lessons to learn are included here.

It must be admitted up front that the vast majority of animals in the Bible wind up in two predictable situations: as someone's dinner or religious sacrifice. We would like to say that "no animals were harmed in the pages of this book," but alas, it would not be true to history or to the story of salvation to present biblical animals as simply pets or merry wild beasts. This is not Disneyland – though at least one snake and one donkey do have the power of speech in Scripture.

Still, we have worked hard not to turn this into a cookbook or how-to manual for burnt offerings. Certainly thousands of animals are sacrificed in the Bible, to which no one objected at the time. God, however, does log some weariness about the whole business of holocaust offerings (see 1 Samuel 15:22; Ecclesiastes 4:17; Isaiah 66:3-4; Hosea 6:6). In the New Testament, Jesus sums up God's disillusionment with ritual sacrifice by saying, "Go and learn the meaning of the words, 'I desire mercy, and not sacrifice'" (Matthew 9:13; see also 12:7). Animal lovers of all ages must cheer at these lines.

The fish and quail here stand in for the dinner-table animals – although these particular specimens are too cute to eat, don't you think? The pigs are happily off the menu in pork-avoiding Israel, but they certainly do not fare well at the end of the story they illustrate. Yet here they seem quite pleased to serve Jesus, even at great personal cost. This makes them better disciples than some of us. The goat and the yearling lamb, each in its own way, bear the weighty responsibility of representing the entire tradition of those sacrificed for the failings of the people – including the Lamb of God himself. Otherwise, the rest of our animals were chosen for their ability to highlight a virtue, symbolize a desirable characteristic, or warn of wickedness. All twenty-six animals share one theme, in that each does God's will – and often more perfectly than we do.

Most of all, we're just having some fun here, and we hope you do too. The best kind of religious education comes about through sneaky catechesis, when we never suspect we're supposed to be learning something. For those who want solid church teaching about our relationship to the animal kingdom, check out the *Catechism of the Catholic Church*, nos. 2415-2418.

A is for the animals that God declared are good.

CITATION: *Genesis, chapter 1*, the story of creation.
Also see *Acts of the Apostles, chapter 10, verses 9-16*, Peter's vision.

LESSONS TO LEARN: *Original blessing. Ecology.*

The creation story is primarily about "original blessing." Some of us learned to equate the creation of the world with original sin, since close upon the heels of creation comes the first act of human disobedience. We may forget that God's intent was to create a *good* place of peace, kindness, and cooperation. Some of us may also have inherited the idea that the material world itself is bad, but God doesn't see it that way. Peter's vision in Acts is a divine reminder that human beings often call things "unclean," but God declares the natural world "clean." We have a responsibility to keep creation clean and healthy, too!

B is for the bear that learns to be a better neighbor.

CITATION: *Isaiah, chapter 11, verses 6-9*, the oracle of the peaceable kingdom.

LESSONS TO LEARN: *The Kingdom of God. Peace.*
The spiritual fruit of self-control.

Bears are described as dangerous beasts in the Bible. We have only to consider the story of Elisha and the heckling boys (in 2 Kings 2:23-25) to see how feared they were! Of the many references to biblical bears, the one in Isaiah's prophecy of the peaceable kingdom shows us how docile even these creatures might be in the better realm God has in mind for us. The bear that learns how to be neighbors with the cow is an example of how we might all learn to be better neighbors – despite our sometimes ferocious natures. A lesson on the nine spiritual fruits (from Galatians 5:22-23) could follow.

C is for the camel that can't fit through narrow places.

CITATION: *Luke, chapter 18, verses 24-39,* the teaching on riches; repeated in *Mark, chapter 10, verses 17-31.*

LESSONS TO LEARN: *Possessions vs. a rich heart. The capital sin of greed.*

We all love stuff – and like the man who comes to Jesus, we spend a considerable part of our lives trying to acquire more of it. But none of our possessions can follow us out of this world. In fact, the more we fasten our hearts on stuff, the harder it may be to let our possessions go. We need our hands and hearts free to hold on to what's truly important – like the hands of the people we are given to love. An exploration of the capital (deadly) sins – pride, jealousy, anger, laziness, greed, gluttony, and obsessive desire – and how they harm our ability to love might spring from this lesson. Like the camel learns, you really can't take it with you.

E is for the elephants that fought in many battles.

CITATION: *I Maccabees, chapter 6, verses 30-37,* an enemy king attacks Israel.

LESSONS TO LEARN: *Free will. God's power vs. worldly power.*

Unlike people who can freely consider and choose their actions, animals rely on instinct. This is why humans are given dominion over the earth's creatures, to provide stewardship and wise discernment. Animals are used as beasts of burden, as co-workers with the farmer, and sometimes as weapons of mass destruction in wartime. Elephants from Asia were trained as fearsome warriors against the armies of Israel, but could not defeat the people loyal to God. In another story, Pharaoh's chariot horses proved no match against God's power, which leads to the saying, "A vain hope for safety is the horse" (Psalms 20:8; 33:16-17; Hosea 1:7).

D is for the dog that walked the road with young Tobias.

CITATION: *Tobit, chapter 6, verse 2, and chapter 11, verse 4,* taking the journey of faith.

LESSONS TO LEARN: *Loyalty. Trust in God. Angel guardians.*

Biblical animals are rarely depicted as pets. Dogs have a particularly nasty reputation, and most references to dogs are intended as insults. Just recall when Jesus says to the woman, "It is not right to take the food meant for children and give it to the dogs" (Mark 7:27; Matthew 15:26). In Tobit, a story originating outside of Israel, the more familiar image of a boy and his dog comes to life. With an ailing father behind him and an uncertain journey ahead, Tobias needs companions to help him find his way. The dog provides the assurances of home, while his other companion turns out to be a guardian angel.

F is for the fish that broke the nets, there were so many.

CITATION: *Luke, chapter 5, verses 1-11,* and also *John, chapter 21, verses 1-11,* stories of the abundant catch; see also *Ezekiel chapter 47, verse 10.*

LESSONS TO LEARN: *God can do what we can't. The mission of the church.*

Fishing all night, with nothing to show for it. We all know how it feels when our hard work seems wasted and frustrated. Then Jesus comes along and suddenly, anything's possible – even the impossible! Sometimes we may think our efforts have led to failure, but God can bring fruitfulness from failure in the blink of an eye. This is a good lesson in God's generous abundance, but also a reminder that what seems a waste of time to us may reap a great harvest in God's sweet time. The great catch of fish also serves as a promise that God will bless the work of the church with divine as well as human power. We don't have to rely solely on what we can do. God can always do more.

G is for the goat that takes the whole town's blame away.

CITATION: *Leviticus, chapter 16, verses 20-28,* the ritual of the scapegoat.

LESSONS TO LEARN: *Actions have consequences. Sin. The sacrament of Penance.*

People do bad things. But that doesn't make them bad people. So what can we do to make things right again when our choices cause trouble between us and others, or between us and God? Choices against love are known as sin, a word that originally meant "missing the mark." When we miss the mark of love, we have sinned. In the Old Testament, the priests of Israel had a ritual to make things right. They confessed the sins of the people and symbolically placed them on a goat. Then they drove the goat into the desert, to show their desire to separate from the choice for sin. Today, the goat is unemployed. We can confess our sins directly to separate ourselves from them.

I is for the insects that will eat when God says, "Eat!"

CITATION: *Exodus, chapters 7-11,* the plagues in Egypt.

LESSONS TO LEARN: *Obedience of creation. Disobedience of humanity.*

When Moses squares off with Pharaoh, it's "smackdown" time in Egypt! Pharaoh has wealth and the power of his throne behind him. Moses has the God of Israel on his side. Ten terrible plagues later, it's obvious this match-up was no contest. In the season of plagues, even insects have roles to play. Although winged insects are called "unclean" in Leviticus 11, that simply makes them unfit to eat. The gnats, flies, and locusts (plagues 3, 4, and 8 respectively) all do their part to remind Pharaoh that creation knows enough to obey its Creator. It takes Pharaoh a long time and a great loss before he is able to learn what a gnat already knows.

H is for the horses that obey the Lord alone.

CITATION: *Book of Revelation, chapter 6, verses 1 to 8,* the riders of Apocalypse.

LESSONS TO LEARN: *God is almighty. Confidence in God's hands.*

The Book of Revelation is misunderstood as a story describing the end of the world. It's better understood as a fifth gospel because, like the gospels, it describes the defeat of evil by the forces of good through Jesus Christ. The difference is that Revelation is written in a symbolic Persian style called apocalyptic. By means of symbols, God's power is revealed and sin is overcome. In the vision of the four horses, the white rider wears a crown (authority), the red one has a sword (power), the black one carries a scale (justice), and the green one brings Death itself. Through this vision, we see that God is entirely in charge and goodness will have the victory.

J is for the jackals. (They take cities that go bad.)

CITATION: *Isaiah, chapter 13, verses 21-22,* jackals take the palaces of Babylon.

LESSONS TO LEARN: *Nature serves God, sometimes better than we do.*

Chances are you don't remember the jackals of the Bible. But they're there, appearing in at least eight places (see also Psalm 44:20; Isaiah 34:13; 35:7; 43:20; Jeremiah 9:10; Lamentations 4:3; and Malachi 1:3) as one of God's go-to animals when cities take the low road and become cruel, hard, and unfair. They are counted among the wild beasts – along with wildcats, owls, ostriches, kites (see K), and even satyrs – to whom God gives over control of cities that have become ghost towns. It's not that God prefers the jackals to be in charge; the truth is that the jackals are ALREADY in charge when societies become uncaring and unjust. Have you ever seen a place where the jackals are in charge?

K is for the kites that will not be without their mates.

CITATION: *Isaiah, chapter 34, verse 15,* when communities sin together.

LESSONS TO LEARN: *The role of the prophet. The idea of collective or social sin.*

Prophecy in the Bible is very often bad news. We don't need prophets to congratulate us when we're doing what's right! God is definitely displeased with human choices in this chapter of prophecy. Edom is selected for punishment, but for us Edom represents any society that embraces a corrupt way of life. How do people sin together? By following bad leaders, by ignoring the needs of the poor, by looking the other way when injustice happens. Kids know well how groups can hurt vulnerable people! When social sin becomes too great, some societies disappear completely. Just ask the kites, small hawks that start their families on ruined cities – and doubtless lent their name to the wind toy.

L is for the lions that spared Daniel in their den.

CITATION: *Daniel, chapter 6,* Daniel is faithful to God in a foreign land.

LESSONS TO LEARN: *Faith, one of three great virtues. Courage, a gift of the Holy Spirit. The capital sin of jealousy.*

In a foreign land, the Jewish youth Daniel remains faithful to God. Daniel's loyalty to God and his favor in the eyes of the king make others jealous of his success. They trick the king into writing a law that would condemn to the lion's den those who pray to anyone but the king himself. Daniel, of course, must disobey this law and the king must throw him to the lions. The king is overjoyed when the lions refuse to harm Daniel, and he throws Daniel's accusers to the lions instead. It's a story about faith – one of the three "theological" virtues along with hope and love. It's also about courage, one of the seven gifts of the Holy Spirit. It also touches on another "deadly" sin, jealousy.

M is for the mice that made the Philistines unhappy.

CITATION: *I Samuel chapters 5 and 6,* the story of the stolen Ark of the Covenant.

LESSONS TO LEARN: *The ark of God. Holy Communion. The tabernacle. Commandments against false gods and stealing.*

Where does God live? In heaven, we might answer. Yes, but where else? God chooses to live in our midst. We believe God's life is literally contained within the elements of our Eucharist. Before the time of Jesus, God's people also believed that God dwelled in the temple in Jerusalem. Even before the temple was built, God's presence was associated with the ark of the Covenant. This special golden box was not something that contained God. Rather, it was a kind of throne on which God's glory "sat" so that people knew God was with them. The Philistines stole the ark from the Israelites and put it in the house with their other gods. Plagues of mice and boils (sometimes translated hemorrhoids or tumors) followed. God's presence and favor cannot be forced.

N is for the nestlings so encouraged by their parents.

CITATION: *Deuteronomy chapter 32, verse 11,* an interesting image of God.

LESSONS TO LEARN: *Images of God.*

"What color is God's skin?" What does God look like, period? We don't know. No one has seen the face of God. It's hard to talk about God when you don't have a clue or even a gender to go by. That's why the Bible gives us images to spark our imagination. God's presence is revealed in a smoking torch, a burning bush, a pillar of fire, a cloud of glory, a Father we can ask for good things, a mother hen gathering her brood, a strong wind and tongues of fire, a lamb of sacrifice, or Jesus himself. Here, God is compared to an eagle encouraging its young in the nest to fly. God is, of course, not wind or fire, not a man or woman, not a bird or a lamb. But we can learn something about God in each of these images.

O is for the ox that let the baby use her manger.

CITATION: *Luke chapter 2, verses 1-20,* the birth of Jesus.
See also Isaiah chapter 1, verse 3.

LESSONS TO LEARN: *The Christmas story. Generosity, one of nine spiritual fruits.*

Christmas carols are full of homey details about "ox and ass lowing" at the crib of baby Jesus. When we examine the gospels, however, we find only Luke and Matthew tell the story of Jesus' birth, and Luke alone describes it in terms of the familiar crèche scene out behind the inn. He doesn't say anything about ox and ass, but that manger must have belonged to some beast of burden. A prophecy from Isaiah supplies these two. The great theme of Christmas is generosity, which Saint Paul calls one of nine spiritual fruits (Galatians 5:22-23). God shows generosity by coming to earth as one of us. The ox, instinctive as animals are, could do no less than to respond with generosity. So do we all at Christmastime.

Q is for the flock of quail that God sent to the desert.

CITATION: *Exodus, chapter 16, verses 1-15,* the flock of quail enter the camp.

LESSONS TO LEARN: *Don't give up. God will provide for us.*

Perseverance is a big word, and some children won't be ready for it. Our teacher used to call it stick-to-it-tive-ness, which was even bigger but more to the point. Forty years in the desert might be a reason to complain, but at this time in the story, Israel hadn't been out there for more than a few weeks. And already they were whining and wanting to go home to Egypt, a land of slavery from which God had just delivered them through amazing signs and wonders! God sends water, bread from heaven, and finally quail to stop their complaining. But they don't stop. How are you when it comes to perseverance? Do you hang in there when things get tough, or quit at the first sign of trouble?

P is for the pigs that ran the demons out of town!

CITATION: *Mark, chapter 5, verses 1-17,* the man freed from his demons.

LESSONS TO LEARN: *Devils and demons. Jesus has power to heal and liberate.*

Devils, like angels, tend to be interpreted literally or dismissed altogether. Kids should know that evil is real. But it's not a Thing Out There that can get us while we sleep. To do right or wrong is a choice we make freely when wide awake. But in the time of Jesus, demons (or devils or unclean spirits) were terms used when people spoke of mental illness or physical sickness that they did not understand. The man who lived in the cemetery was probably mentally ill, and people were so afraid of him they did not want him to live in their village. Yet no sickness of mind or body or spirit was too great for Jesus to deal with. He freed this man, because God wants us to be whole and happy.

R is for the ravens that brought food to good Elijah.

CITATION: *1 Kings, chapter 17, verses 1-6,* the prophet Elijah exiled to the desert.

LESSONS TO LEARN: *The prophet's job is telling the truth.*

The stories of the early prophets – Elijah and his replacement Elisha – are full of hair-raising adventures and near-miss escapes. From the contest with the priests of Baal at Mount Carmel to his departure from this world on a fiery chariot, Elijah in particular captures the religious imagination. Although we usually think of prophets as holy men who wrote books of prophecy, the early prophets were primarily truth-tellers and miracle workers. In this episode, Elijah becomes so unpopular after predicting a drought that God decides to send him into the "witness protection program" in the desert. With a stream nearby and ravens bringing take-out, God provides for the one who speaks the truth.

S is for the sheep that's lost – and Jesus brings him home.

CITATION: *Luke, chapter 15, verses 1-7,* the 100th sheep. See also *Matthew, chapter 18, verses 1-14,* and *John, chapter 10, verses 1-16.*

LESSONS TO LEARN: *Jesus is the friend of the lost.*

When it comes to Jesus, playing the friend card is not always a good idea. Children know what a friend is, and Jesus is clearly not someone to play with. Nor is it helpful to reduce our Lord and Savior to yet another imaginary, invisible friend. Kids really need grownups to be grownups! Every child, too, knows the fear of being lost, and the relief and joy of being rescued. Jesus is *that* kind of friend: the friend in need. Saint Anthony might find your lost items, but what about when YOU'RE the one who's lost? Turn to Jesus. It's not just that he'll help you find your way home when you're literally lost. He'll help you return to the person God made you to be, even when you think that person's gone for good.

And if there WAS a Unicorn, he must have missed the boat....

CITATION: None. There are no unicorns in the Bible. Or anywhere else, for that matter.

LESSONS TO LEARN: *The relationship between the Bible, history, and science.*

Obviously, we're just having some fun here. There are no animals in the Bible that start with the letter U. And there are no unicorns because, as far as we know, there never were any. But kids often ask, "Why are there no dinosaurs in the Bible?" Answer: Their bones had not yet been discovered or recognized. Paleontology and many other branches of science were not yet known or in very primitive practice two or three thousand years ago, when most of these stories were written down. There ARE mythical beasts in Scripture: Leviathan and Rahab, both sea monsters, and many dragons appear. The Bible does not pretend to be the history of the world, but *salvation history* – the history of the people of faith.

T is for the turtledoves heard cooing through the land.

CITATION: *Song of Songs, chapter 2, verses 11-13,* the time for love. See also *Ecclesiastes chapter 3, verses 1-8,* a season for everything.

LESSONS TO LEARN: *God is love. Love is therefore a gift from God.*

At last, a lesson on love. While the Song of Songs is primarily a poem about romantic love, the church has long used it as a metaphor for the love God has for the human race. Is it hard to imagine God as a lovesick boy or a girl swooning with desire – for you and for me? Maybe we can't believe it because our desire for God is not nearly as strong. But our faith tells us God became one of us, lived and suffered and died for us. How does the story of Jesus make any sense without the idea that God is crazy about us? Spring is the season when the love song of the turtledove reminds us that the world is new again. It's a new chance to take God's love seriously. And to share it with those whom we love.

V is for the vipers that resemble nasty folks.

CITATION: *Matthew chapter 3, verse 7; chapter 12, verse 34;* and *chapter 23, verse 33,* the brood of vipers.

LESSONS TO LEARN: *Hypocrisy. Being true, inside and out.*

John the Baptist was the first to use the term "brood of vipers" when referring to false religious leaders. Jesus liked the image enough to employ it himself. The brood of vipers weren't just people doing bad things, but people who pretended to be good while really doing wrong! I asked third graders once what you call someone who pretends to be one thing but is really another. They immediately volunteered the word hypocrite. Kids learn this one early – often, sad to say, from the example of adults. What may be less familiar is the idea of integrity: being true to yourself inside and out. We don't want to look or act like a bunch of snakes! We want to be true like Jesus.

W is for the great big whale that swallowed Jonah whole.

CITATION: See the *Book of Jonah, especially chapter 2,* in the belly of the fish.

LESSONS TO LEARN: *Doing God's will and not ours. Mary's yes to God.*

The story of Jonah is not about a historical person. It was written to describe what happens when we insist on having things our way and not God's way. God's will is always better than ours, because God has a better view of the world than we do. The best example of someone who did it God's way is Mary, the mother of Jesus. She said, "Let it be done to me according to your will." (Luke 1:38) But the prophet Jonah didn't want to do what God willed. He wanted things his way, and his way was definitely not to bless the enemies of his country! Mary ends up with Jesus in her belly. Jonah ends up in the belly of a great fish....until he learned to do it God's way.

Y is for the yearling lamb that gave his life like Jesus.

CITATION: *Exodus, chapter 12,* the yearling sacrifice; see also *Revelations, chapter 21, verses 22-27,* the triumph of the Lamb.

LESSONS TO LEARN: *The meaning of sacrifice. The season of Lent. The Way of the Cross.*

Sacrifice is a hard concept even for grownups to accept. Why should we give things up, as we do during Lent? Why do parents give up freedom and ease to make room for children? Why do soldiers fight and die for their countries? Why should we send our money away to help others in need? The yearling, or year-old lamb, gives its life to save the households of Israel during the final great plague in Egypt. The blood of the lamb protects each family from death. In the same way, Jesus is the "Lamb of God" who takes away the sin of the world. He offers his life for ours, just like the yearling lamb. Saving others often costs a great price, but God will reward those who make a sacrifice.

X is for the extra-special donkey that could talk!

CITATION: *Numbers, chapter 22, verses 2-35;* see also *chapters 23 and 24,* Balaam the prophet.

LESSONS TO LEARN: *Blessing and cursing. Pleasing God is better than pleasing people.*

If everything you said out loud actually happened, you would probably become very careful with your words! As truth tellers, the prophets held power because their words, inspired by God, took effect. This made a prince of Moab want to hire the prophet Balaam to pronounce a curse over his enemy, the Israelites. A curse is a kind of evil fortune-telling. Balaam sets out to do it, but God's angel bars the road. Balaam, a prophet who's listening to a prince instead of to God, can't see the angel – but his donkey sure can! The donkey tells his master not to beat him for being stubborn. He's the only animal since the snake in Eden that can talk. Balaam decides to bless Israel instead of cursing them.

Z is for the zebra pair that made it just in time.

CITATION: *Genesis chapter 6, verse 5, through chapter 9, verse 17,* the story of the great flood.

LESSONS TO LEARN: *God loves creation and promises to rescue it. God is just.*

Were there zebras in the Middle East? For the sake of argument, let's say that they came a long way to get on that boat. The mother of all flood stories doesn't have a lot of interior consistency, so fudging the details here is not a problem. We see strains of two different versions poking through the surface. How many animals boarded the ark? Two of each, or seven pairs of some? How long did the flood last? Forty days, or a year and eleven days? In any case, the details are not historical. This is a story about the relationship between God's love for creation and God's justice in the face of evil. Our God is a God who saves, but God is also just and will not permit wickedness to rule the earth.